# BOSS OF THE PLAINS

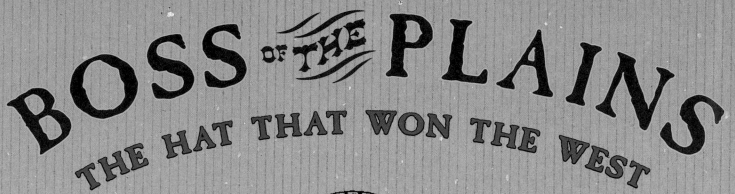

## THE HAT THAT WON THE WEST

by Laurie Carlson

pictures by Holly Meade

A DK INK BOOK

DK Publishing, Inc.

**A**t first, settlers and travelers in the American West wore whatever hats they had worn back home: knit caps, wool derbies, or straw sombreros.

Some wore old sea captain's caps; others wore army hats, calico sunbonnets, homburgs, slouch hats, or even silk high hats.

Everyone wore some kind of hat, though, because the weather was likely to be either burning sunshine, drenching rain, whipping wind, or swirling snow. A hat was important protection.

One hat would come along that was particularly well suited to frontier life. This is the true story of that amazing hat—the hat that won the West.

In the 1840s, while explorers pushed on through new territory and pioneers tamed the mountains and plains of the West, twelve-year-old John Batterson Stetson sat on a high wooden stool, working along with his father and his eleven brothers and sisters in the family's tiny, damp hatmaker's shop in Orange, New Jersey.

The Stetsons made hats the same way hatters had done it for years: by pressing felt, made from wet fur and wool, over a wooden form to shape it.

John sat at the worktable and dreamed of the West he'd heard customers and neighbors talk about.

Out west there were clear skies, roaming buffalo, and the promise of adventure. Everyone seemed to be going there. Everyone except hatmakers.

It wasn't until years later, when the dampness and steam of the shop had weakened his lungs and he became sick with tuberculosis, that John Stetson decided to go west himself. If he wanted to see the West, he couldn't wait. So he headed to the town where the West began: St. Joseph, Missouri, the jumping-off point where people bought gear and supplies for their journey to the goldfields.

It was 1859, and St. Joe's streets were bustling and crammed with wagons, mules, pack dogs, and adventurers bound for the frontier.

Determined to start a new life in St. Joe, John looked around for some way to make his mark. It was only when he met up with a group of travelers heading to Colorado Territory that opportunity presented itself.

"Why not come to Pikes Peak with us?" they asked. "There's gold there, and fortunes to be made."

That was all John Stetson needed to hear.

It was a 750-mile trip, and the long days of walking in the dry prairie air soon improved John's health. Before long his legs grew strong and he hardly ever coughed.

One night the Pikes Peakers huddled around their campfire.

"Sure wish we had a snug tent," one of the travelers commented. "Maybe we could make one out of the rabbit skins we've been saving."

"Won't work," someone else replied. "The skins will shrink up and get hard unless they're properly tanned."

John Stetson smiled. "Fur can be made into cloth without tanning," he announced.

"Can't be done!" the others scoffed.

But John knew that it could. He'd been making hats that way
for years. So he spread out a blanket and gathered the dried
rabbit pelts, along with a hatchet, a canteen of water,
and a hickory sapling. He put the kettle on to boil.

He carefully shaved the fur from the first hide
and piled it in the center of the blanket.

Then he sliced a strip of hide off
the rabbit skin and tied each end
of the strip to the hickory stick. It
looked like an Indian's bow.

Next he flicked the bow, blowing puffs of
fur up in the air to settle back down on the
blanket until they made an even layer.

As everyone watched, John took a swig from the canteen
and gently sprayed water through his teeth onto the fur
until it matted.

With a gleam in his eye, he carefully lifted the corner of the fur; it came up off the blanket in one piece. Then he walked to the campfire and dipped the piece of matted fur in and out of the boiling water until it shrank into a little blanket.

"Felt!" he proclaimed. "Thick, warm, and stronger than a piece of cloth." It had worked!

Soon John and his friends were sleeping warm and snug in a new felt tent.

Over a month later, the Pikes Peakers reached the gold hills of Colorado. They eagerly went from diggings to diggings, trying their luck.

The scorching sun blistered John's face, and the whipping wind blinded him. The short brim of his derby hat, so stylish back in New Jersey, gave him no protection at all.

Before long John decided to make a better hat for himself. "Big and picturesque," he declared, and set to work, using the same technique he'd used to make his tent. It felt good to be making a hat again.

At first the other miners teased John about his funny hat. It certainly was different from the hats back home and the ones they wore. It had a wide brim and a tall crown and was made of thick fur felt. But it worked. The brim kept the sun out of John's eyes and the rain off his back. And when it got dirty, the tough felt could be brushed or thumped to knock the dust off.

One day a horseman rode into camp. When he saw John's unusual hat, his eyes lit up with excitement.

To everyone's amazement, he reached into his pocket, pulled out a five-dollar gold piece, and offered to buy the hat right off John's head!

Delighted, John pocketed the coin. Back in New Jersey, even the finest hat sold for just two dollars. He grinned and waved as the stranger rode out of camp wearing his distinctive hat.

Pickings in the Colorado goldfields were slim, and after a year of digging, John had little money to show for it. But he still had a trade and talent. He decided to move to Philadelphia to do the one thing he really knew how to do: make hats.

At first he made the styles that were most popular back east, but so did all the other hatters. John wanted to make something unique, something special—a hat that everyone would notice. He even made up styles of his own and wore the hats to drum up orders, but no one in the city was interested.

John Stetson was determined to succeed. He remembered the horseman out west who had thought that his high-crowned, wide-brimmed hat was just right. Maybe other Westerners would like it, too—bullwhackers, who drove oxen; mule skinners, who led mule teams; and drovers, who herded cattle or sheep. He'd make a hat for the wranglers and cowboys of the West. And he knew just what he'd name his new hat:

John spent what little money he had left from mining gold on materials for sample hats. He made them all the same: of light tan felt, with a wide brim, a high crown, and a plain band. He packed sample hats and order forms in special boxes and sent one to every clothing store and hat dealer in the West. Then he waited.

——————◆——————

Two weeks passed. Nothing happened. John sat in his empty shop thinking about the gamble he had taken. Had he wasted his time and all his money? Had he been foolish to think anyone would buy his unusual hats?

But then, all at once, orders began pouring in. Each day's mail brought more. People wanted the hats. In fact they wanted them right away, and they had stuffed money into the envelopes to make sure they got them quickly.

John used the money to buy supplies and began turning out hats as fast as he could. Out west, cowboys tossed away their knit caps, sombreros, and derbies. In no time, John B. Stetson's Boss of the Plains became the most popular hat west of the Mississippi.

Even though the Boss of the Plains
cost a cowboy a whole month's wages,
it was worth it.

It shielded a cowpoke's eyes
from blinding sun and caught the
rain before it trickled down his back.

It could wave cows into a corral . . .

or fan the flames of a newly lit campfire.

It could be used to carry oats to feed a
horse or to scoop up a refreshing drink of
water from a cold mountain stream.

It could impress a lady at the Saturday night dance . . .

or come in handy when the sweetest huckleberries were ready to be picked.

It was the perfect decoy when a cowboy was in trouble . . .

and made a soft cushion for a cowboy's head at the end of a hard day.

Westerners laughed about this hat they liked so much. They often said, "It gets so you can smell it across a room, but you just can't wear it out."

John Stetson had become an important part of the great American adventure called the West. Others had done it by striking gold, blazing trails through unknown territory, or taming a wild land. He made his mark with a hat.

# John Batterson Stetson

## May 5, 1830 – February 18, 1906

John B. Stetson's hats spread across the West—and the world—like wildfire. His hat company began to make other styles, too, and soon it seemed that everyone, not just cowboys, wanted a Stetson hat. U.S. presidents, marshals, marines, rangers of the Forest Service, and the Texas Rangers all wore Stetsons. The Royal Canadian Mounted Police and European royalty wore them, too. Famous rodeo cowboys and western movie stars like Buffalo Bill, Annie Oakley, Calamity Jane, and the Lone Ranger came to Philadelphia to have their hats fitted. They held rodeos and Wild West shows on the factory grounds for the workers and their children.

To keep up with the demand for hats, Stetson expanded his factory; it eventually grew to twenty-five buildings, filling a whole city block. He made sure that his employees had a clean, safe place to work, and he built a hospital, a park, and houses for the five thousand workers of the John B. Stetson Company.

Even today you can buy a Stetson hat. There are dozens of styles, but the Boss of the Plains is still being made—in Missouri now, where John Batterson Stetson first began his journey west.

# For Terry, Ed, and John—L.C.

## BIBLIOGRAPHY

Blevins, Winfred. Dictionary of the American West. New York: Facts on File, 1993.

Botkin, B. A. A Treasury of Western Folklore. New York: Crown, 1951.

Cybriwski, Roman A., and Charles Hardy III. "The Stetson Company and Benevolent Feudalism." Pennsylvania Heritage (Spring 1981): 14–19.

Foster-Harris, William. The Look of the Old West. New York: Viking, 1955.

Hat Brands, Inc. How Hats Are Made. Garland, Texas: Hat Brands, Inc., n.d.

Henderson, Debbie. Cowboys and Hatters: Bond Street, Sagebrush, and the Silver Screen. Yellow Springs, Ohio: Wild Goose Press, 1996.

"John B. Stetson Dead." The New York Times (February 9, 1906).

Lycan, Gilbert. The Stetson Story. DeLand, Florida: Stetson University, 1977, revised 1993.

Miller, Fredric M., Morris J. Vogel, and Allen F. Davis. Still Philadelphia: A Photographic History, 1890–1940. Philadelphia: Temple University Press, 1983.

"Mr. John B. Stetson." Florida Baptist Witness (August 27, 1964): 11.

Stetson Hat Company. "The Stetson Century, 1865–1965." St. Louis, Missouri: Stetson Hat Company, 1965.

"Stetson Ran His Workers' Lives." The Philadelphia Inquirer (April 16, 1991): 21–A.

"The Stetson Story." American Heritage (Spring 1953): 28–31.

Time-Life Books. The Old West Series: The Cowboys. New York: Time-Life Books, 1973.

A BIG THANK YOU for helpful advice and information to the following: Susan Hengel, Hagley Museum and Library, Wilmington, Delaware; John Rosenthal, president, and Jeralyn Rice, Hat Brands, Inc.; Dr. Debbie Henderson; Anne Wheeler, National Cowboy Hall of Fame, Oklahoma City, Oklahoma; Jean Zajac, librarian, New Jersey Historical Society; Autry Museum of Western Heritage, Los Angeles; Louis Waddell, Pennsylvania Historical and Museum Commission, Harrisburg; Michael Sherbon, Pennsylvania State Archives; the John B. Stetson Company; Tom Stetson, Coeur d'Alene, Idaho; Gail Grieb, Stetson University, DeLand, Florida; and the helpful staff at Boot Barn, Spokane, Washington. Hats off to you all!

A Melanie Kroupa Book

**DK Ink**

DK Publishing, Inc., 95 Madison Avenue, New York, New York 10016

Visit us on the World Wide Web at http://www.dk.com

Text copyright © 1998 Laurie Carlson
Illustrations copyright © 1998 Holly Meade
Stetson, John B. Stetson, and "Boss of the Plains" are trademarks of the John B. Stetson Company, Mt. Kisco, New York, for hats and other products, used by permission herewith.
The photograph of John Stetson on page 31 is used by permission of the Autry Museum of Western Heritage.

Library of Congress Cataloging-in-Publication Data

Carlson, Laurie M.
    Boss of the plains : the hat that won the west / by Laurie Carlson ; illus. by Holly Meade.
        p.    cm.
    "A Melanie Kroupa book."
    Summary: The story of John Stetson and how he came to create the most popular hat west of the Mississippi.
    ISBN 0-7894-2479-7
    1. Stetson, John Batterson, 1830–1906—Juvenile literature.   2 Hatters—United States—History Biography—Juvenile literature.   3. Hat trade—History—Juvenile literature. [1. Stetson, John Batterson, 1830–1906.   2. Hatters.   3. Hats.] I. Meade, Holly, ill. II. Title.
    HD9948.U62S7425    1998                                              97-30995
    338.7'6874'092—dc21                                                    CIP
    [B]                                                                          AC

Book design by Chris Hammill Paul. The text of this book is set in 17 point Caslon Antique.

Printed and bound in the United States of America

First Edition, 1998

2  4  6  8  10  9  7  5  3  1

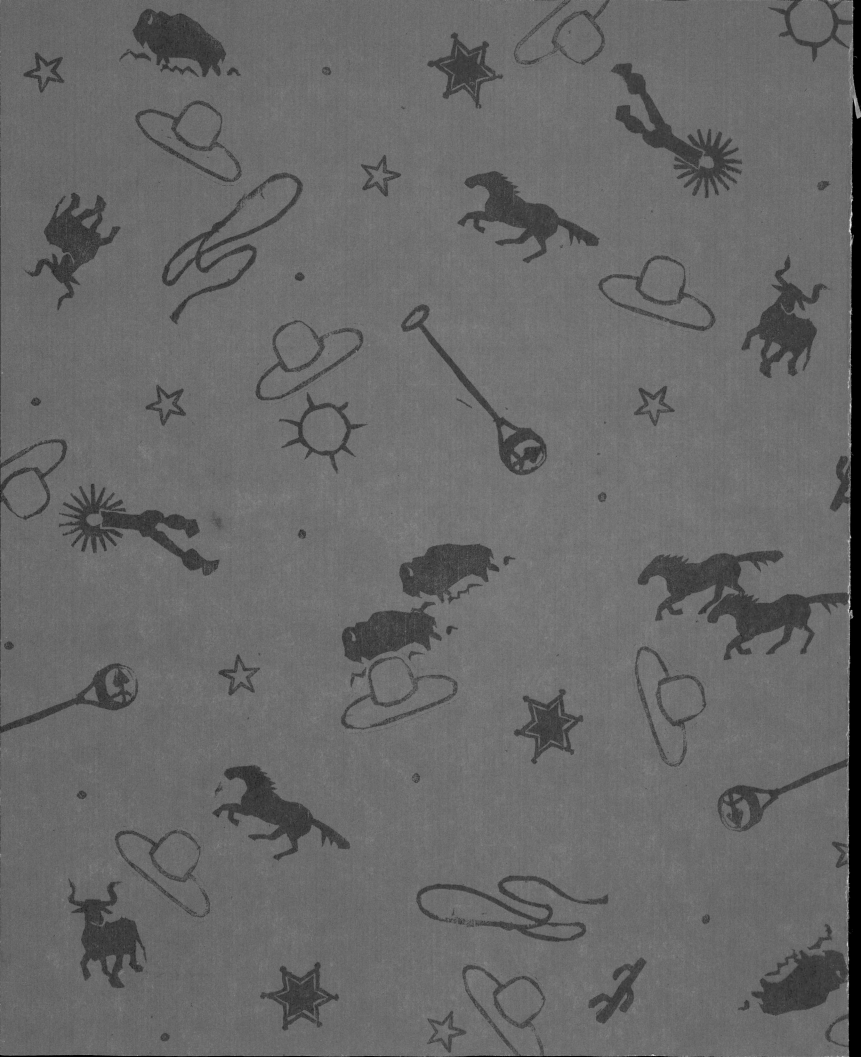